Senses

KINGFISHER

Kingfisher Publications Plc
New Penderel House
283–288 High Holborn
London WC1V 7HZ
www.kingfisherpub.com

First published by Kingfisher Publications Plc 2004
2 4 6 8 10 9 7 5 3 1

1TR/0504/PROSP/RNB(RNB)/140MA/F

A CIP catalogue record for this book is
available from the British Library.

ISBN 0 7534 0928 3

Editor: Catherine Brereton
Senior designer: Peter Clayman
Cover designer: Poppy Jenkins
Picture research: Rachael Swann
Illustrations: Sebastien Quigley (Linden Artists)
DTP co-ordinator: Sarah Pfitzner
Artwork archivists: Wendy Allison, Jenny Lord
Senior production controller: Oonagh Phelan
Indexer and proof-reader: Sheila Clewley

Printed in China

Acknowledgements
The Publisher would like to thank the following for permission to reproduce their material.
Every care has been taken to trace copyright holders. However, if there have been unintentional omissions or failure
to trace copyright holders, we apologize and will, if informed, endeavour to make corrections in any future edition.
b = bottom, c = centre, l = left, t = top, r = right

Photographs: 1 Corbis; 2–3 Michael K. Nichols/National Geographic; 4–5 Raymond Gehman/National Geographic; 6–7 Alamy Images;
9r Digital Vision; 10cl Adam Hart-Davis/Science Photo Library; 10–11b Sean Murphy/Getty Images; 12l Piers Cavendish/ardea.com;
12–13t DiMaggio/Kalish/Corbis; 13br Jeff Lepore/Science Photo Library; 14bl NHPA/James Carmichael Jr; 14–15tc NHPA/Stephen Dalton;
15br NHPA/Nigel J Dennis; 17br Susumu Nishinaga/Science Photo Library; 18l Mark Baker/Reuters; 18–19b Roy Morsch/Corbis; 19tr Tony
Marshall/EMPICS Sports Photo Agency; 20l NHPA/William Paton; 20–21c NHPA/Daryl Balfour; 21br Duncan McEwan/Nature Picture Library;
22bl(l) Joel W. Rogers/Corbis; 22bl(r) Nick Gordon/ardea.com; 22–23t NHPA/ANT Photo Library; 23br Georgettte Douwma/Getty Images;
24bl NHPA/Stephen Dalton; 25tr NHPA/ANT Photo Library; 25br Dietmar Nill/Nature Picture Library; 26l Craig Hammel/Corbis;
27t BSIP VEM/Science Photo Library; 27br Suzanne & Nick Geary/Getty Images; 28tl François Gohier/ardea.com; 28–29b NHPA/Guy
Edwardes; 29tr NHPA/Ann & Steve Toon; 30–31b Pascal Goetgheluck/ardea.com; 31tr John Downer Productions/Nature Picture Library;
31br Roy Morsch/Corbis; 32br Corbis; 33b Omikron/Science Photo Library; 34l NHPA/Martin Harvey; 34–35b NHPA/T Kitchin & V Hurst;
35tr Matthew Oldfield, Scubazoo/Science Photo Library; 37tl Phil Jude/Science Photo Library; 38l Angelo Cavalli/Getty Images
and Ryan Mcvay/Getty Images; 38–39b NHPA/Kevin Schafer; 39tr Dr Jeremy Burgess/Science Photo Library;
48 Ralph A. Clevenger/Corbis.

Cover photography by Daniel Pangbourne.
Commissioned photography on pages 33, 36 and 42–47 by Andy Crawford.
Project-maker and photoshoot co-ordinator: Miranda Kennedy.
Thank you to models Corey Addai, Anastasia Mitchell,
Sonnie Nash and Shannon Porter.

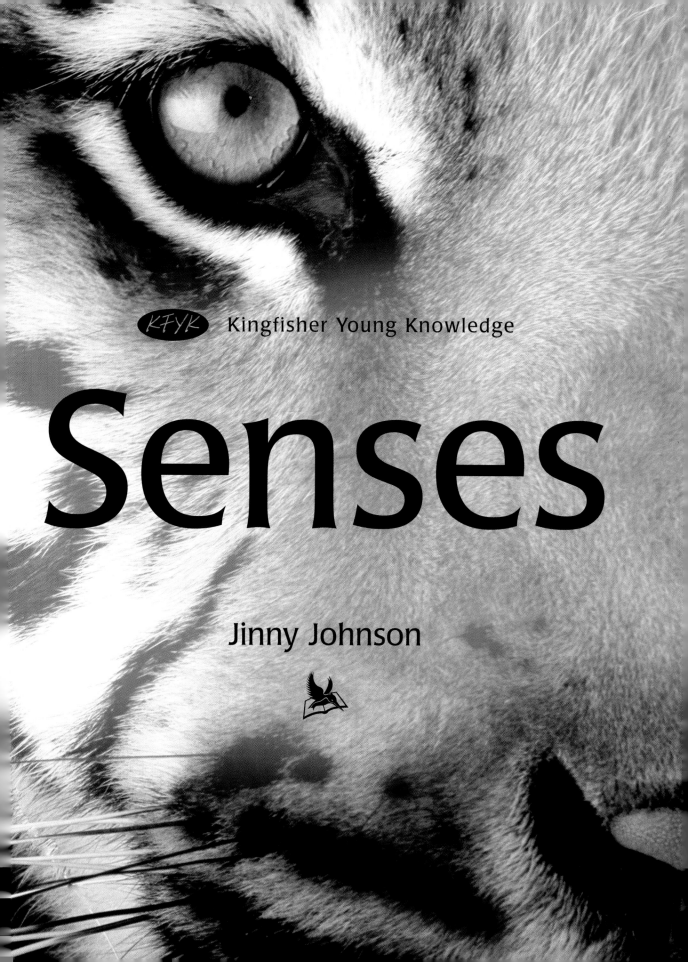

KFYK Kingfisher Young Knowledge

Senses

Jinny Johnson

Contents

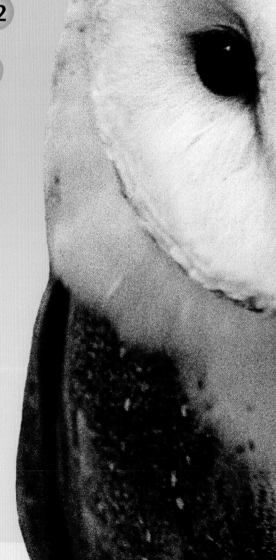

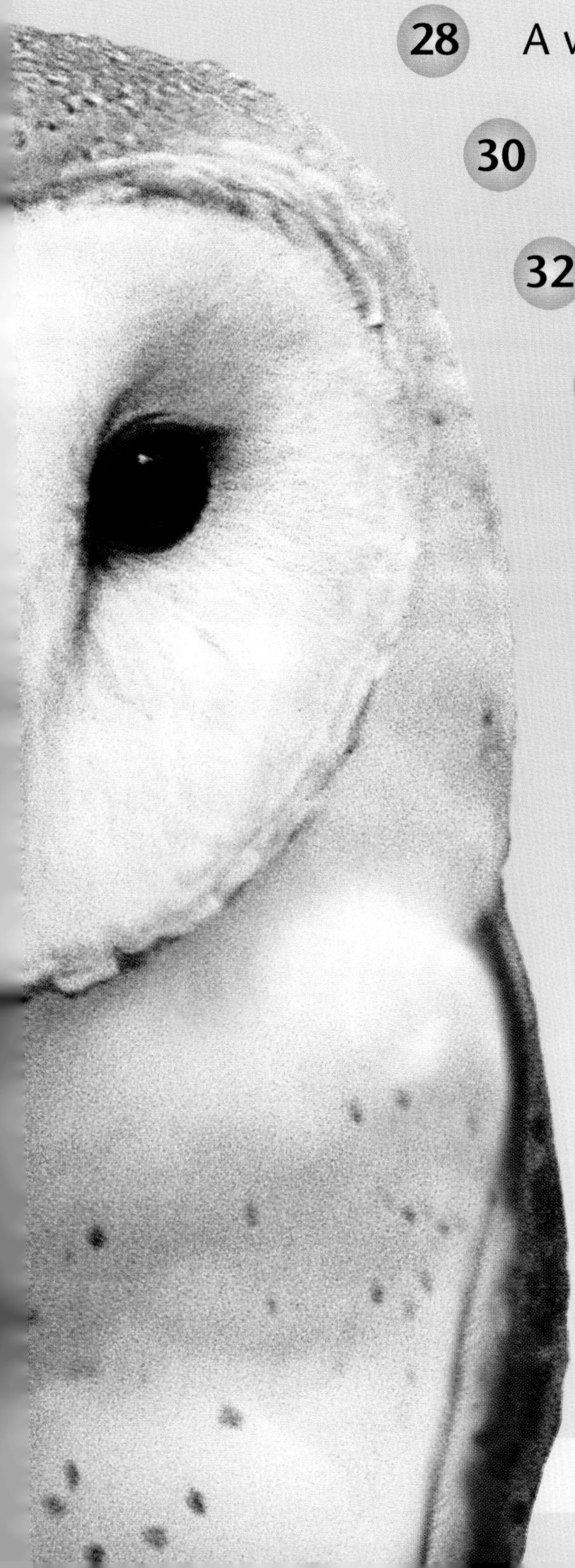

What are senses?

Imagine the world if you could not see things or hear your friends talking, or if you could not smell and taste your food. We do not often think about our senses, but they tell us what is going on around us. We have five main senses. These are sight, hearing, smell, taste and touch.

Super senses

Animals have senses too. Some animals have better senses than we do. Dogs can hear sounds that humans cannot, and they have a much stronger sense of smell.

Using senses

This boy can see his pet's big brown eyes, feel his soft fur and hear his snuffling sounds. He can also smell the roses in the background and can probably smell his dog.

The sense centre

brain

Your brain controls your senses. Messages travel from your eyes, ears, nose, tongue and skin to tell it what is going on. The messages travel along special pathways in the body called nerves.

Messages to the brain

Nerves go from the brain to all parts of your body. A message can zoom along the nerves to the brain in a tiny fraction of a second.

nerves

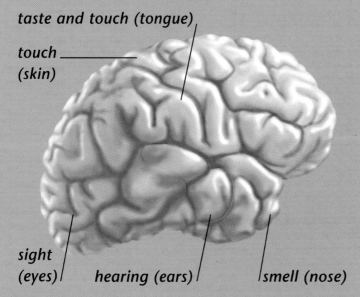

taste and touch (tongue)

touch (skin)

sight (eyes)

hearing (ears)

smell (nose)

Jobs for the brain

The brain sorts out the messages it receives from the nerves. Look at the picture on the left to see which parts of the brain sort out messages to do with your senses.

nerves – special structures like wires that run from the brain to all parts of the bo

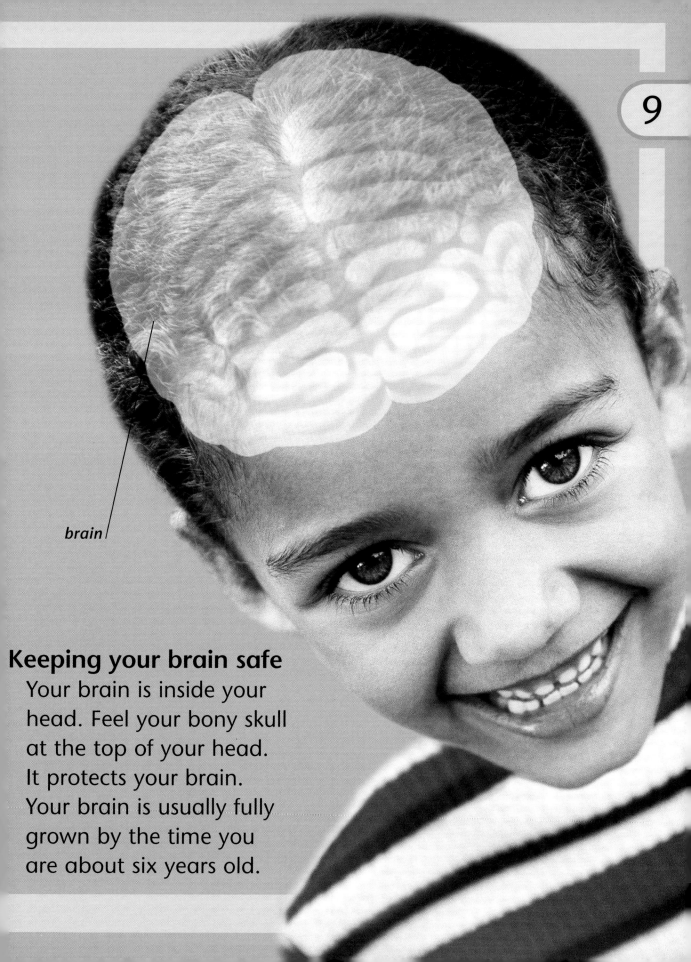

brain

Keeping your brain safe

Your brain is inside your
head. Feel your bony skull
at the top of your head.
It protects your brain.
Your brain is usually fully
grown by the time you
are about six years old.

How do I see?

Your eyes make pictures of the outside world – a bit like a camera does. You can see big things and small things, and you can see lots of different colours.

pupil (black)
iris (brown)

Letting in light

The black circle at the centre of your eye is called the pupil. This is an opening through which light passes into your eye.

Eye colour

The coloured part of the eye is called the iris. It can be blue, green or brown. What colour irises do these children have?

lens – *part of the eye that focuses light*

Making a picture

When you look at something, light bounces off it and goes into your eye. Inside the eye the lens makes an image on the area called the retina, at the back of the eye. Messages about this image travel along nerves to the brain.

iris

pupil

lens

retina

nerve

bone in eye socket

Amazing eyesight

Some animals have excellent eyesight. Their eyes need to be right for the job they have to do – such as spotting food or looking out for danger.

Night eyes

Hunting animals, such as this cat, have powerful, forward-facing eyes that help them see detail well and judge exactly where something is. Cats can see much better at night than we can.

Sharp sight

Birds of prey, such as this peregrine falcon, can see things from a long way away. Its large, alert eyes can spy a tiny mouse from high up in the air.

All-round view

Side-facing eyes help this mouse see as much of what is going on around it as possible. This means it can spot any enemies – and has a chance to escape!

prey – *an animal that is hunted and eaten by other animals*

Different eyes

Not all animals have eyes quite like ours. Some animals have eyes that look very different, but are perfect for helping them find food.

Spider eyes

Most spiders have eight eyes. But only the two large eyes at the front are used for seeing. The smaller ones pick out any movement and help the main eyes find prey.

Two directions

The chameleon stays very still as it watches for insects to catch. Its big bulgy eyes can swivel around and even point in two directions at once.

Mini eyes

A dragonfly's eye is made up of 30,000 parts. Each one is like a tiny eye. These let the dragonfly see lots of images at high speed so it can track fast-moving prey.

chameleon

wivel – *turn around on one spot*

How do I hear?

Your ears allow you to hear sounds, from a quiet whisper to the loudest pop music. The outside parts of your ears pick up sounds and funnel them down inside your ears.

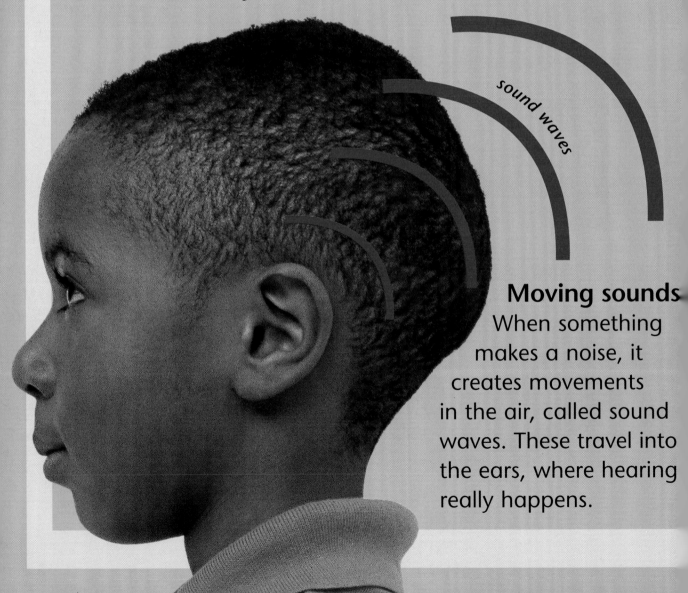

sound waves

Moving sounds
When something makes a noise, it creates movements in the air, called sound waves. These travel into the ears, where hearing really happens.

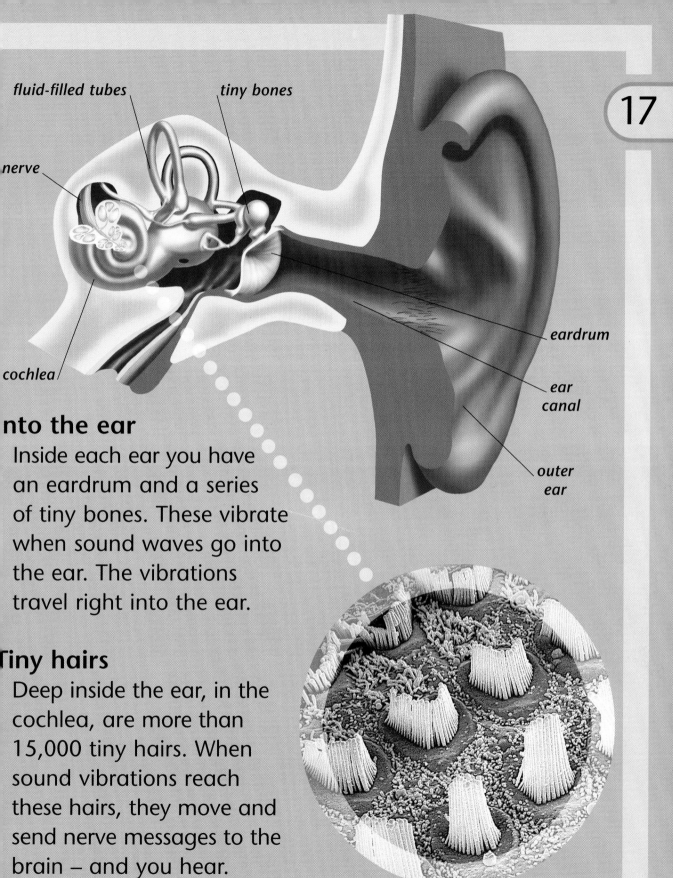

fluid-filled tubes

tiny bones

nerve

cochlea

eardrum

ear canal

outer ear

Into the ear

Inside each ear you have an eardrum and a series of tiny bones. These vibrate when sound waves go into the ear. The vibrations travel right into the ear.

Tiny hairs

Deep inside the ear, in the cochlea, are more than 15,000 tiny hairs. When sound vibrations reach these hairs, they move and send nerve messages to the brain – and you hear.

ibrate – move rapidly to and fro

Keeping balanced

As well as allowing you to hear sounds, your ears help you to keep your balance. As you move around, tiny hairs in fluid-filled tubes in your ear tell you which way up you are.

Travel sick

You may feel sick on a boat because your brain gets confused. Your ears tell it you are moving but your eyes say you are not.

Dizzy spells

If you spin around, then suddenly stop, your ears do not get the message to your brain straight away. You feel this as dizziness.

Practice makes perfect

Gymnasts do not get dizzy because they practise their moves over and over again so that their brains get used to the signals.

Animal ears

Ears come in all shapes and sizes. The ears of the African elephant are the biggest of all. They can be two metres long.

Listening for danger

The rabbit's long ears help it catch the tiniest sound that might mean danger is near. It can also swivel its ears to pick up sounds from different directions.

Far away calls

Elephants can hear much deeper sounds than we can. They can hear the low calls of other elephants from several kilometres away.

Insect ears

Some insects have ears in surprising places. Crickets have ears on their front legs. This grasshopper has its ears on each side of its body.

Listening underwater

The ocean may look like a silent world, but it is not. Sounds travel further through water than air, and fish, whales and other creatures can hear sounds.

Closed ears

An otter does not use its ears underwater. When it dives, it closes its ears so it will not get water in them.

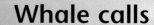

Whale calls

All you can see of a whale's ears is a tiny hole on each side of its head. But whales have excellent hearing. A humpback whale can hear the calls of other whales from many kilometres away.

humpback whale

Listening fish

Fish have ears inside their bodies that allow them to hear what is going on around them. They make noises to keep in touch with each other and listen for sounds of enemies – or food!

Sound pictures

Bats, whales and dolphins are some of the creatures that have a special sense called echolocation. This means that they use sound instead of sight to make a 'picture' of their surroundings.

Night hunters

Bats hunt at night and can catch an insect in total darkness by using echolocation. As it flies, the bat makes lots of very high sounds. . .

echo – sound that bounces off an object

'Seeing' sounds

Echolocation works in water, too. Dolphins find food in the deep, dark ocean by making sounds that echo and help them 'see' their prey.

Sound echoes

. . . When the bat's sounds meet an insect, they make echoes that bounce back to the bat's ears. The echoes tell the bat where its prey is, how big it is and even how fast it is moving.

Smelling things

Your sense of smell happens inside your nose. Most of the outside of your nose is to do with warming and cleaning the air you breathe in before it travels to your lungs.

A-tishoo!

You sneeze when something irritates the inside of your nose and your body tries to force it out. The tiny hairs in your nose trap dust and dirt, and stop it getting into your lungs.

How you smell

When you smell something, tiny bits of its scent travel into your nose. They go right to the top into two special sense areas. Nerves send messages from there to your brain, telling it about the smell.

lungs – *two large spongy bags in your chest that you use for breathing*

A world of smells

For some creatures, the sense of smell is more important than sight. Many animals smell their enemies before they see them. Predators often hunt by smell.

Super nose

Bears have a very keen sense of smell to help them find food. A polar bear can smell its prey from 20 kilometres away.

Life in the dark

Moles live underground, where it is so dark that eyes are not much use. A mole finds its way around by its senses of smell and touch.

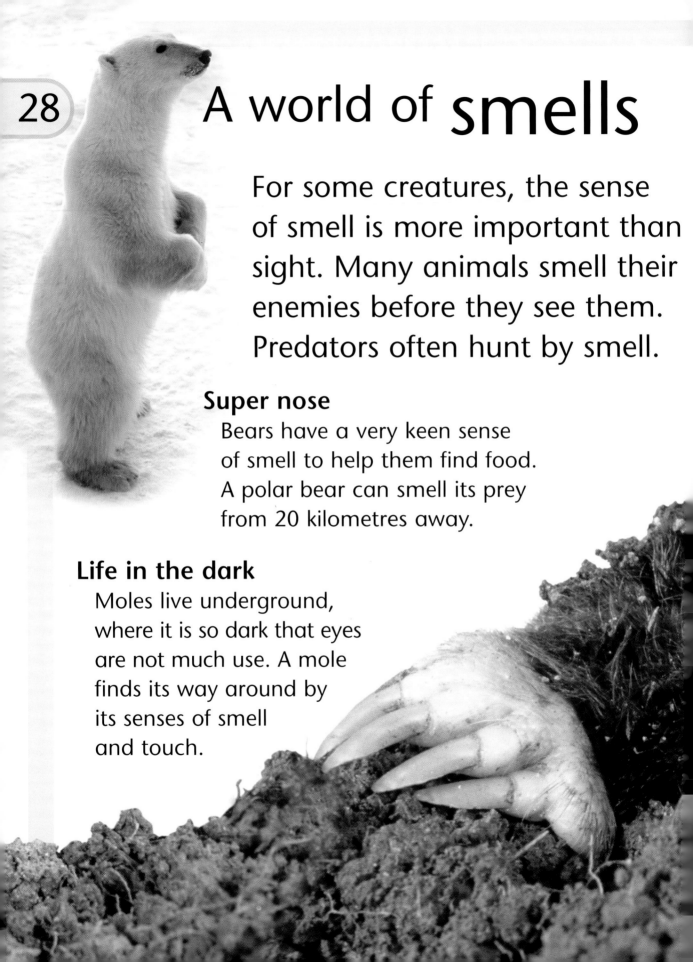

Smell check

Deer take a break now
and then from feeding
on grass, and look up
to sniff the air for any
signs of danger.

Smelly messages

Many animals use smell to send messages to each other. These might say 'Keep away' or 'I am looking for a mate'. When a dog sniffs a tree it can tell which other dogs have marked the spot.

Special signals

When a female moth is ready to mate she gives off a special scent. The feathery antennae on a male moth's head can pick up the smell from five kilometres away.

Smelly warning

The skunk uses smell to protect itself. If an enemy comes too close, the skunk squirts out a very smelly liquid from an area near its tail, to warn it off.

My mark

When a cat rubs its cheeks against something, it is leaving a scent message. It is saying 'I was here. This is my patch.'

32 Tasting things

Your sense of taste works with your sense of smell to tell you about the food you eat. You taste with your tongue. Taste helps you enjoy food, but also warns you if something is not good to eat.

Four flavours

There are four main flavours: bitter, salty, sour and sweet. Most foods are a mixture of more than one of these. Different areas of the tongue are sensitive to certain flavours. Match the colours below to the picture opposite to see where these are.

bitter

salty

sour

sweet

Taste buds

Your tongue is covered with about 10,000 tiny taste buds, which are too small to see. Each taste bud is sensitive to a particular kind of taste.

sensitive – able to feel or taste

Bumpy tongue

Your taste buds are clustered around the little bumps you can see on your tongue. Nerves inside the taste buds send messages to your brain about what you are tasting.

Animal tastes

Like us, animals have taste buds on their tongues, but it is hard to know just what they taste. Most probably use smell and taste to tell what is good to eat.

Good taste

Tigers – and pet cats – have sensitive tongues. They can taste different flavours in ordinary water.

Swimming tongues

Catfish are like swimming tongues – they have taste buds on their bodies, which help them find food in the water. They can also taste food with their whiskers, called barbels.

Tasting toes

Butterflies taste with their feet as well as with their mouths. This way, they know what kind of food they have landed on before they unroll their tongues to eat.

Touch and feel

You can feel with any part of your body because your skin contains lots of tiny nerve endings. These send messages to the brain about what you are touching.

soft

What does it feel like?

When you hold something, notice how it feels. It may be rough or smooth, sharp or soft, hot or cold. Our sense of touch tells us these things. It also lets us feel pain.

cold

sharp

smooth

hot

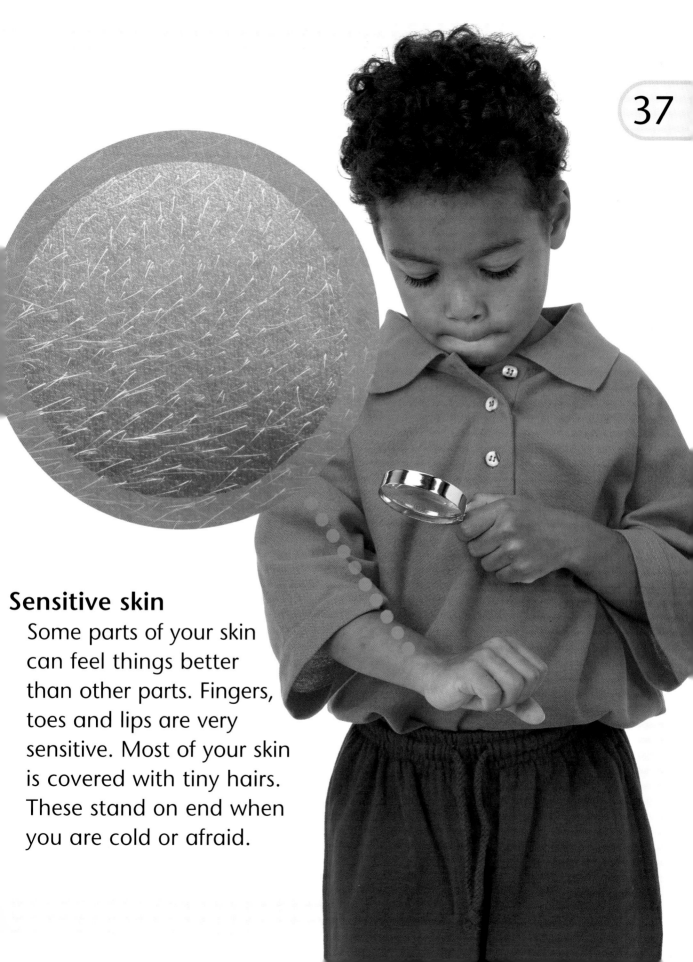

Sensitive skin

Some parts of your skin can feel things better than other parts. Fingers, toes and lips are very sensitive. Most of your skin is covered with tiny hairs. These stand on end when you are cold or afraid.

Animal touch

Animals feel things with their skin too. But some have extra ways of touching. Many animals have very sensitive whiskers, which help them find out about their surroundings.

Super trunk

The tip of an elephant's trunk is the most sensitive part of its body. It does lots of things with its trunk, from stroking its young to picking up tiny leaves.

whiskers – *long hairs on an animal's face*

Hairy legs

A spider waits on its web for its prey. Hairs on the spider's legs sense the tiniest movement that might mean food is near.

Wet paws

The raccoon has very sensitive paws as well as whiskers. They are even more sensitive when wet, which may be why the raccoon wets its paws before eating.

Which line is longer?
Seeing involves your brain as well as your eyes. Sometimes your brain can be tricked into seeing something that is not really there.

You will need
- Paper
- Coloured pen or pencil
- Ruler

1

Using your ruler, draw a straight line 9cm long. Draw another 9cm line beside the first line, about 5cm away.

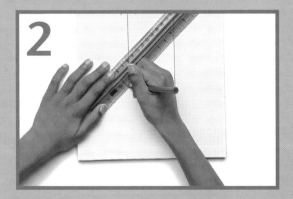

2

On the first line, draw arrowheads pointing inwards. On the second line, draw arrowheads pointing outwards, as shown in step 3.

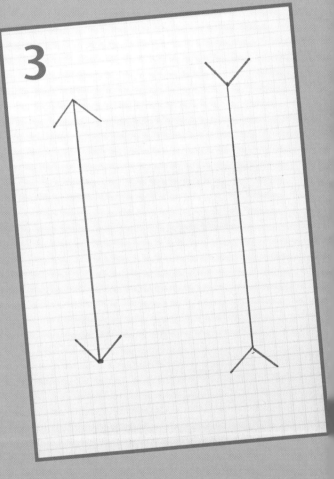

3

Look at the straight lines. Does one look longer than the other? The directions of the arrowheads trick your brain into thinking that one line is longer than the other.

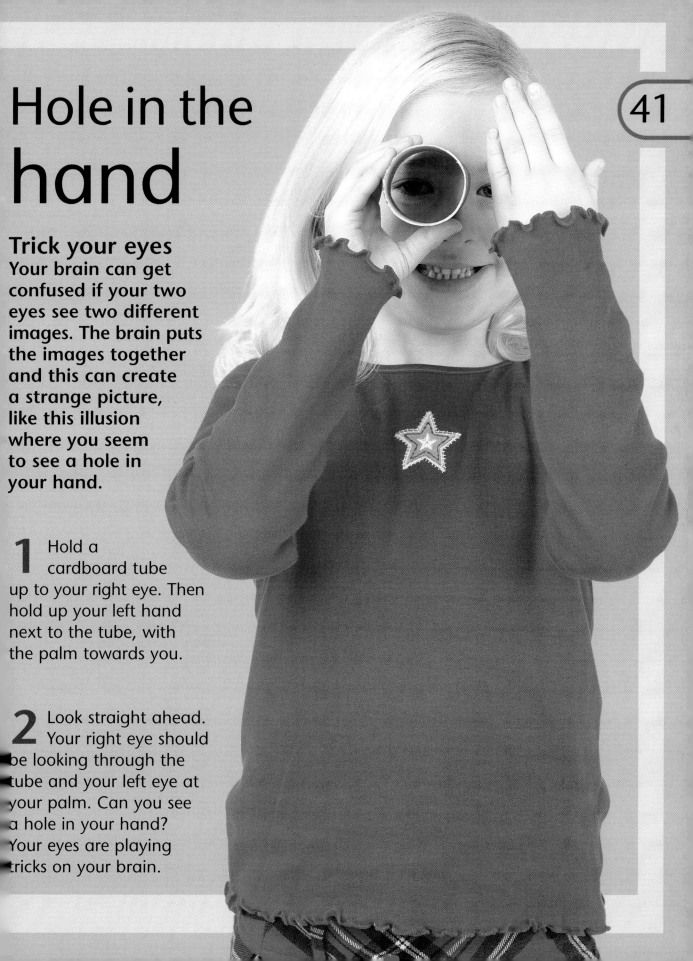

Hole in the hand

Trick your eyes

Your brain can get confused if your two eyes see two different images. The brain puts the images together and this can create a strange picture, like this illusion where you seem to see a hole in your hand.

1 Hold a cardboard tube up to your right eye. Then hold up your left hand next to the tube, with the palm towards you.

2 Look straight ahead. Your right eye should be looking through the tube and your left eye at your palm. Can you see a hole in your hand? Your eyes are playing tricks on your brain.

Model eardrum

How hearing works

Make a loud noise and you will see the stretched balloon on your model eardrum vibrate just like your real eardrum does.

You will need
- Balloon
- Scissors
- Plastic cup
- Elastic band
- Rice grains

Use scissors to cut the neck off a balloon. Then carefully cut down one side so that you can open the balloon out flat.

Cut the opened-out balloon in half so you have a piece big enough to fit over the top of your plastic cup. This will be the eardrum itself.

Stretch the balloon over the cup. Fix it on with the elastic band, keeping the balloon stretched as tightly as possible.

Sprinkle some rice grains on top of the balloon. Clap your hands or shout. Watch the grains jump as the stretched balloon vibrates.

Listening game

What can you hear?
Find a quiet spot and play this game – you will be surprised at the number of different sounds you hear.

You will need
- Notepad
- Pen

Sit down with your notepad and pen. Listen carefully for sounds – a noisy lorry, birds singing or a dog barking. Write down or draw pictures of the things you hear.

Taste and smell

Guess the smell

You will be surprised at how difficult it is to tell what things are without looking at them, using just your sense of smell.

You will need
- Scarf
- 5 plastic cups
- 5 smelly things: we used vinegar, a bun, chocolate, banana and toothpaste

Ask a friend to sit down, and tie a scarf over his eyes. Make sure it is tight enough that he cannot see, but not so tight that it hurts.

Add one smelly thing to each plastic cup. Then hold the first cup under your friend's nose and ask him to take a good sniff.

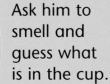

Ask him to smell and guess what is in the cup.

Give him the other foods to smell one by one. See how many he can get right. Some smells are easy to guess, while others are harder.

Guess the taste

Try guessing different drinks by taste alone. It can be difficult when you cannot see them, especially if some are similar.

You will need
- Scarf
- 5 plastic cups
- 5 drinks: we used milk, chocolate milk, orange juice, apple juice and water

As with the smelling game, ask a friend to sit down, and tie a scarf over her eyes. Make sure she is comfortable but cannot see.

Pour five different drinks into the plastic cups. Make sure you ask an adult which drinks you can use.

Ask your friend to take a sip of the first drink and guess what it is. Ask her to try each in turn, and see how many she gets right.

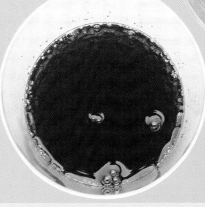

Make a touch cube

Test your touch

This is a fun way to test your sense of touch. When you have made the cube, you can play with it or play a touch guessing game.

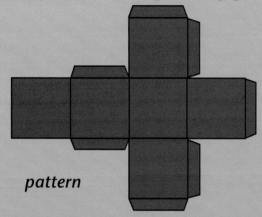

pattern

To make your touch cube you will need to cut a piece of card in the pattern shown above. You might need to ask an adult to help you copy it.

You will need

- Stiff card
- Pen
- Scissors
- Card square
- Ruler
- Glue
- 6 different textured items: we used velvet, corrugated card, cotton wool pad, kitchen foil, sandpaper and cereal shapes

Place your card square on the stiff card. Draw around it six times to make the pattern. Add flaps where shown in the pattern.

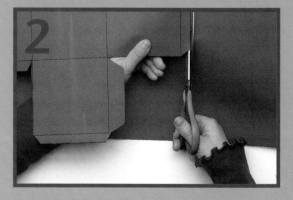

Carefully cut around the outside of the pattern, keeping all the edges as straight as you can. Then fold along all the lines.

3

Hold the middle square down with your finger and fold up the sides to make a box shape. Glue down the flaps to stick the box together.

4

Take some cereal shapes and carefully glue them to one side of the box to make a rough texture. You can use any kind you like.

5

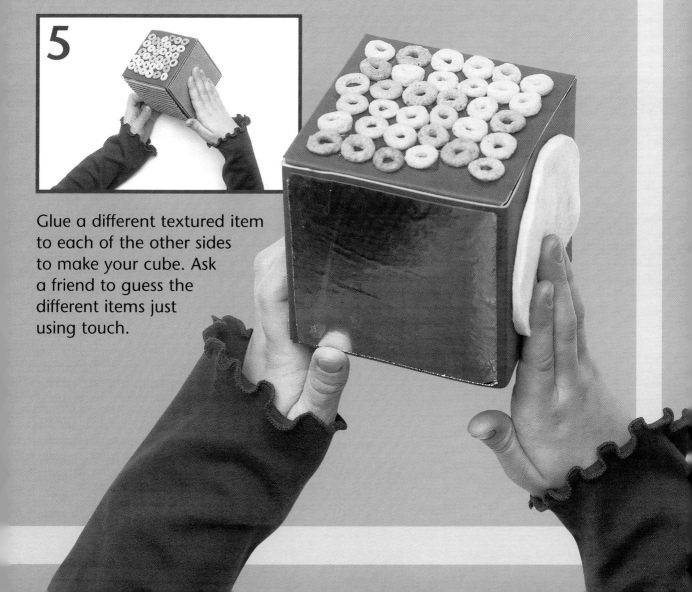

Glue a different textured item to each of the other sides to make your cube. Ask a friend to guess the different items just using touch.

Index